FINGERPICKING
Praise

T004083Z

ISBN 978-0-634-09891-8

Visit Hal Leonard Online at www.halleonard.com

HAL•LEONARD®
CORPORATION
7777 W. BLUEMOUND RD. P.O. BOX 13819 MILWAUKEE, WI 53213

INTRODUCTION TO FINGERSTYLE GUITAR

Fingerstyle (a.k.a. fingerpicking) is a guitar technique that means you literally pick the strings with your right-hand fingers and thumb. This contrasts with the conventional technique of strumming and playing single notes with a pick (a.k.a. flatpicking). For fingerpicking, you can use any type of guitar: acoustic steel-string, nylon-string classical, or electric.

THE RIGHT HAND

The most common right-hand position is shown here.

Use a high wrist; arch your palm as if you were holding a ping-pong ball. Keep the thumb outside and away from the fingers, and let the fingers do the work rather than lifting your whole hand.

The thumb generally plucks the bottom strings with downstrokes on the left side of the thumb and thumbnail. The other fingers pluck the higher strings using upstrokes with the fleshy tip of the fingers and fingernails. The thumb and fingers should pluck one string per stroke and not brush over several strings.

Another picking option you may choose to use is called hybrid picking (a.k.a. plectrum-style fingerpicking). Here, the pick is usually held between the thumb and first finger, and the three remaining fingers are assigned to pluck the higher strings.

THE LEFT HAND

The left-hand fingers are numbered 1 through 4.

Be sure to keep your fingers arched, with each joint bent; if they flatten out across the strings, they will deaden the sound when you fingerpick. As a general rule, let the strings ring as long as possible when playing fingerstyle.

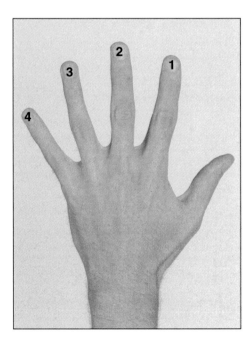

Breathe

Words and Music by Marie Barnett

Drop D tuning:
(low to high) D–A–D–G–B–E

Intro
Moderately

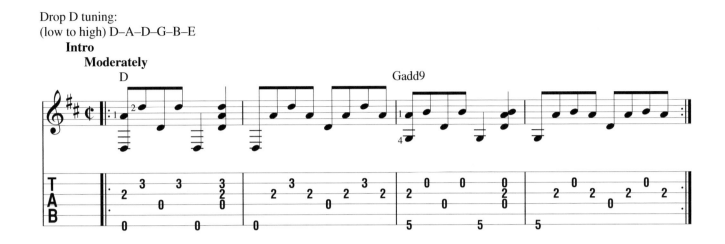

Verse

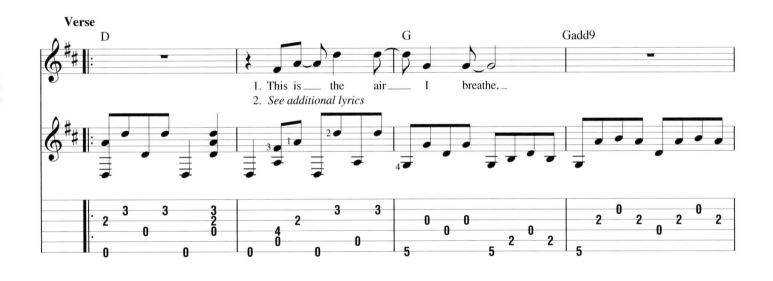

1. This is ___ the air ___ I breathe, ___
2. *See additional lyrics*

this is ___ the air ___ I breathe, ___

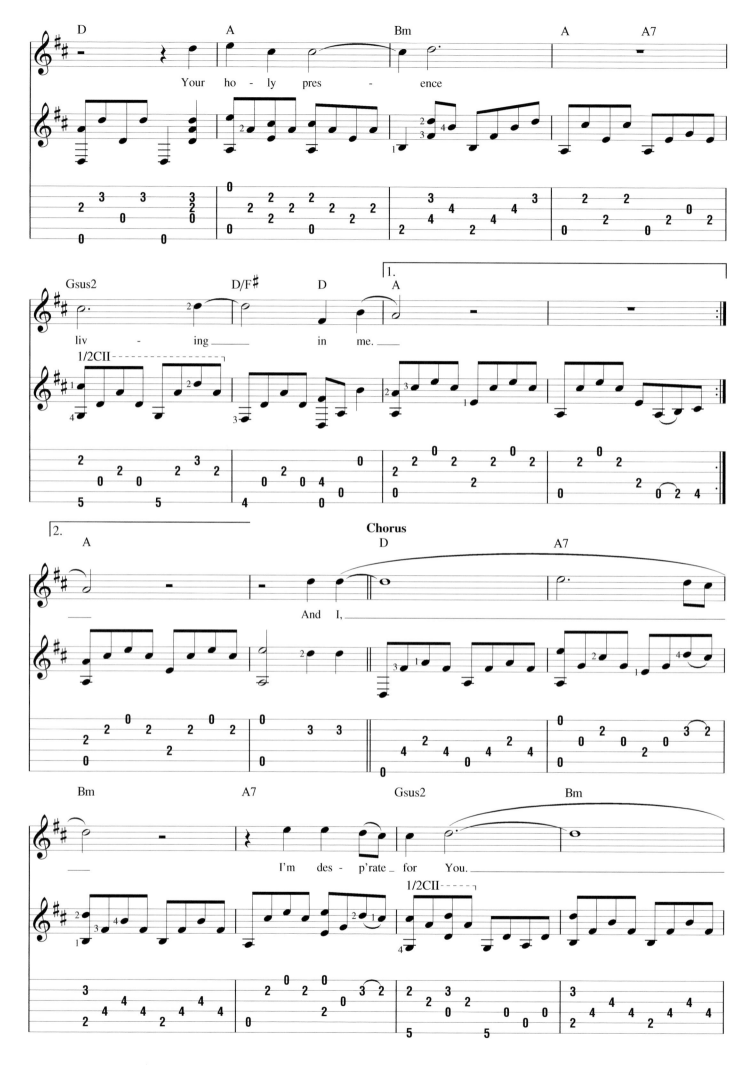

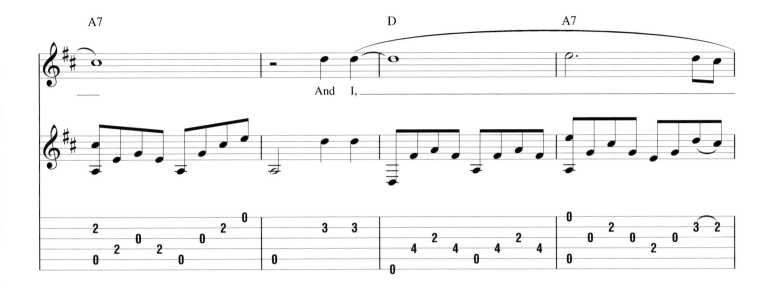

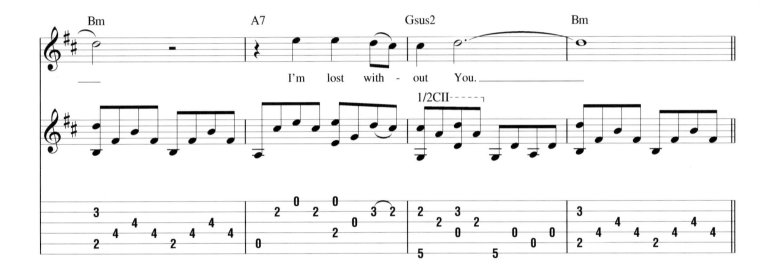

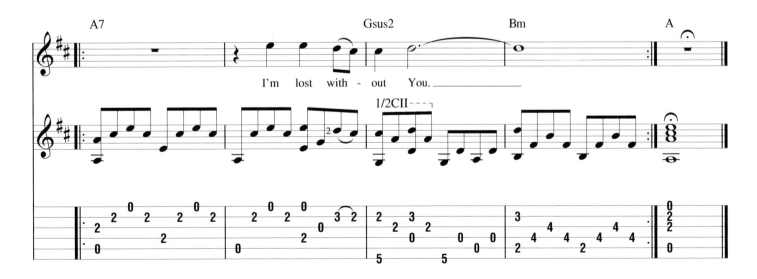

Additional Lyrics

2. This is my daily bread,
   This is my daily bread,
   Your very Word spoken to me.

Above All

Words and Music by Paul Baloche and Lenny LeBlanc

Drop D tuning:
(low to high) D–A–D–G–B–E

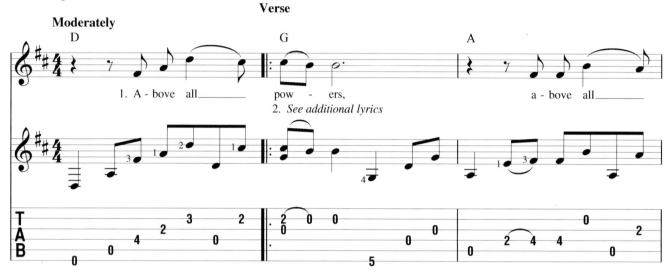

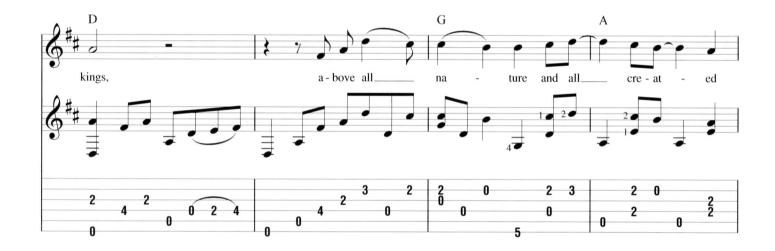

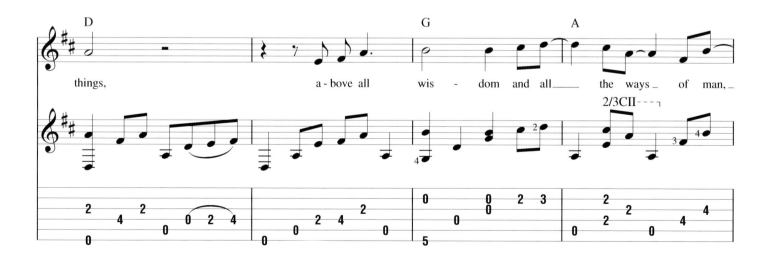

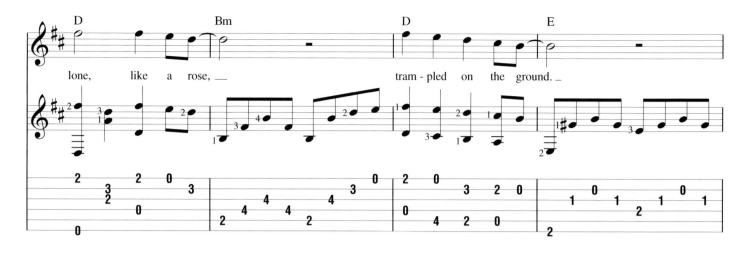

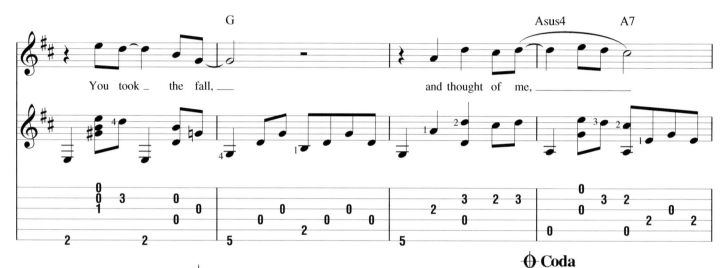

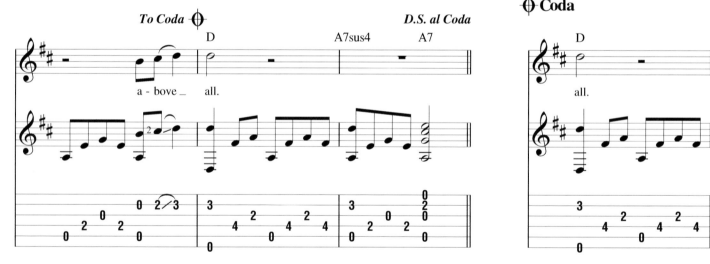

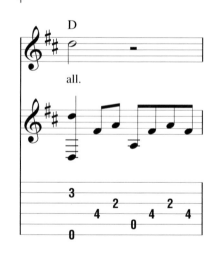

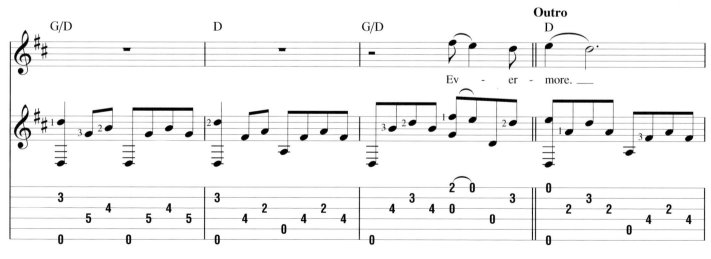

Additional Lyrics

2. Above all kingdoms, above all thrones,
   Above all wonders the world has ever known,
   Above all wealth and treasures of the earth,
   There's no way to measure what You're worth.

Draw Me Close

Words and Music by Kelly Carpenter

Drop D tuning:
(low to high) D–A–D–G–B–E

Verse
Slowly

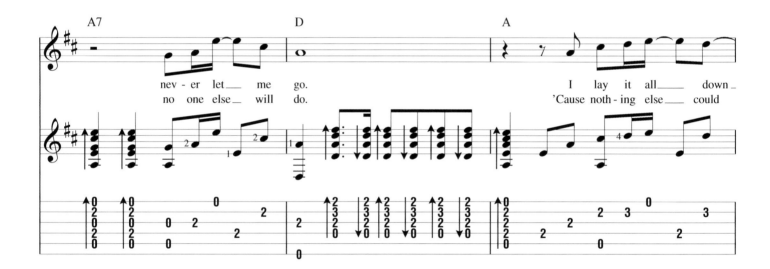

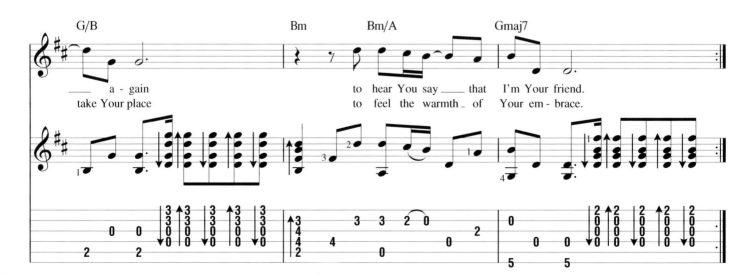

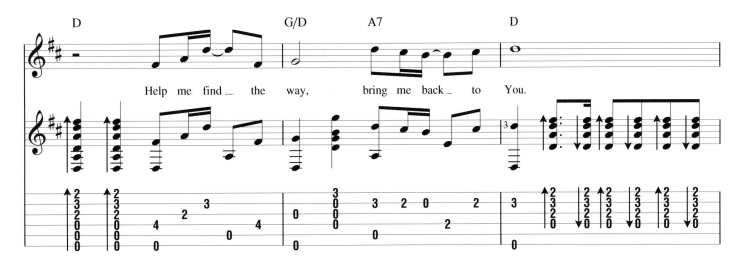

Help me find __ the way, bring me back __ to You.

Chorus

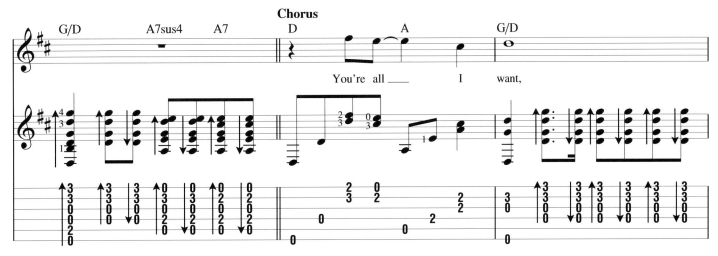

You're all __ I want,

You're all __ I've ev-er need -ed. You're all __ I

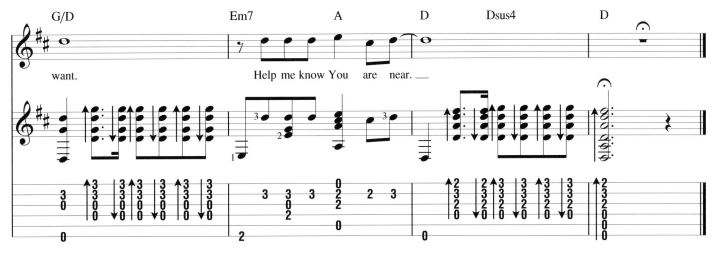

want. Help me know You are near. __

Give Thanks

Words and Music by Henry Smith

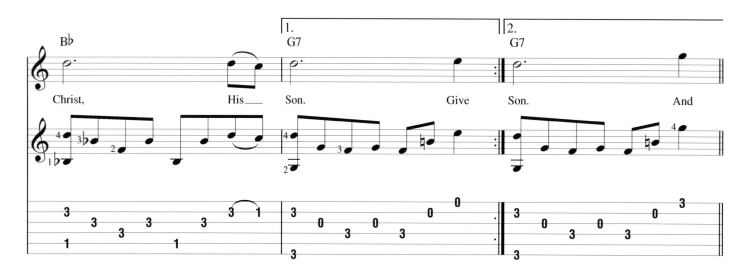

Chorus

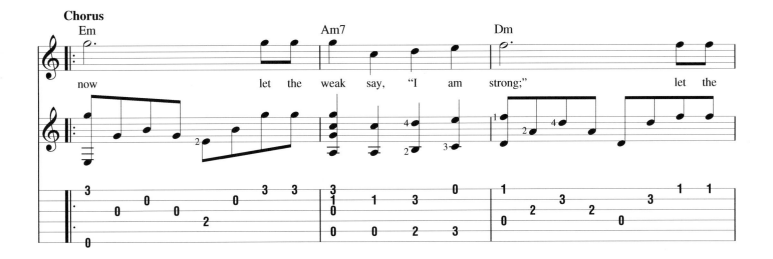

now   let the weak say, "I am strong;"   let the

poor say, "I am rich," _____ be - cause of what the Lord has

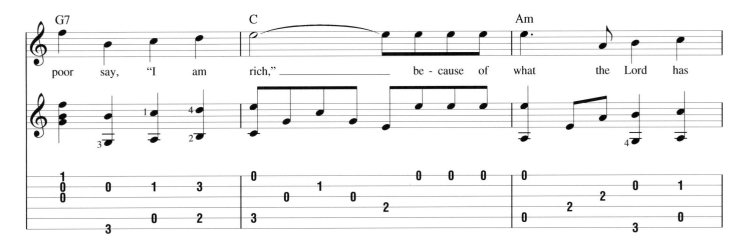

done   for ___ us.   And us.   Give

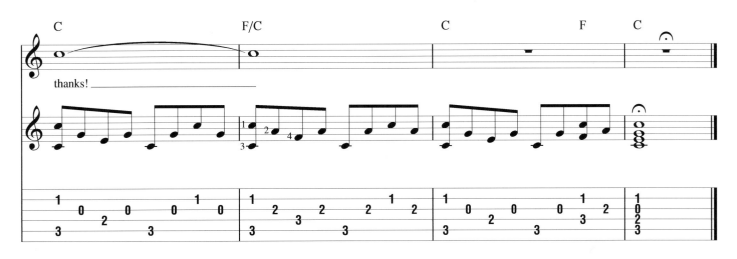

thanks! _____

Great Is the Lord

Words and Music by Michael W. Smith and Deborah D. Smith

Drop D tuning:
(low to high) D–A–D–G–B–E

Verse

Moderately slow

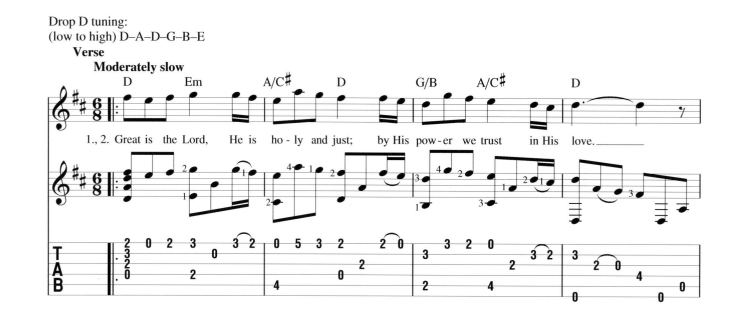

1., 2. Great is the Lord, He is ho-ly and just; by His pow-er we trust in His love._____

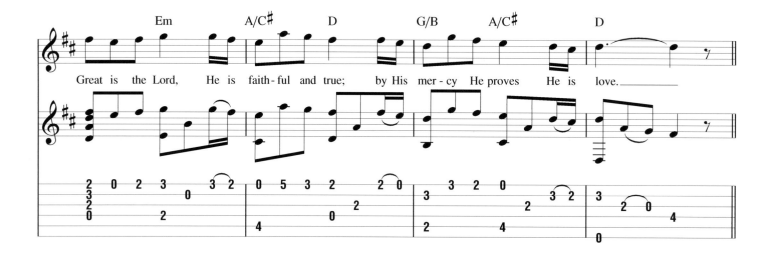

Great is the Lord, He is faith-ful and true; by His mer-cy He proves He is love._____

𝄋 Chorus

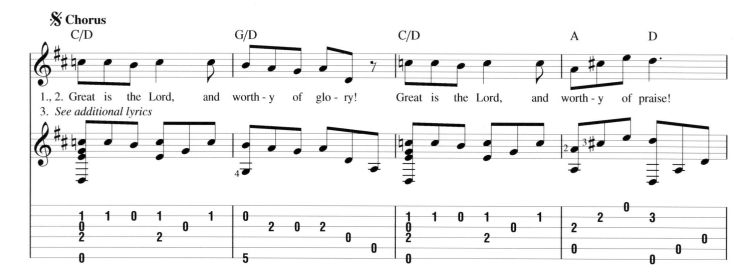

1., 2. Great is the Lord, and worth-y of glo-ry! Great is the Lord, and worth-y of praise!
3. *See additional lyrics*

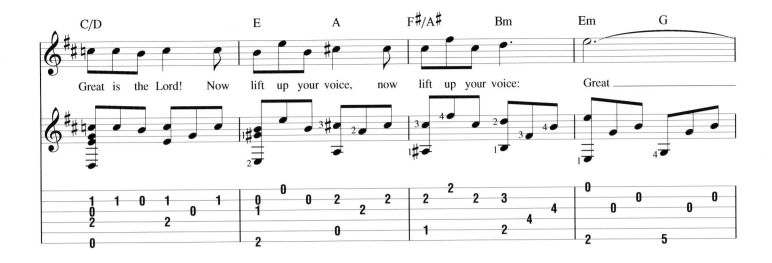

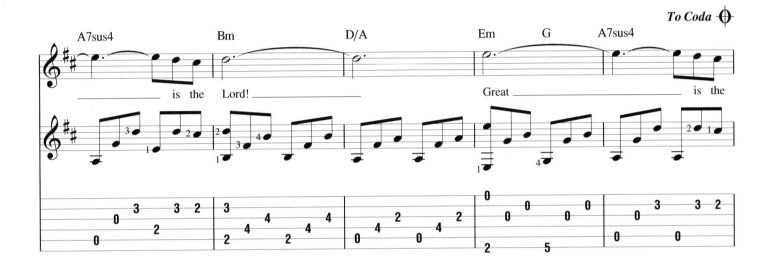

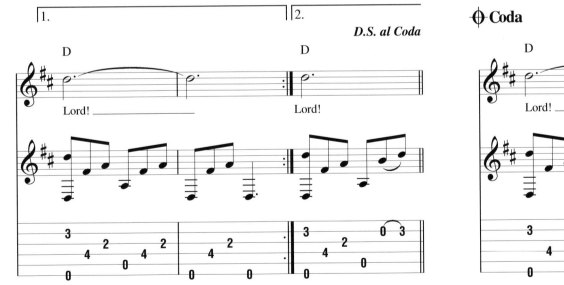

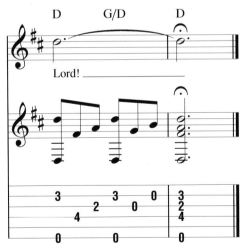

Additional Lyrics

Chorus 3. Great are You, Lord, and worthy of glory!
Great are You, Lord, and worthy of praise!
Great are You, Lord! I lift up my voice,
I lift up my voice:
Great are you, Lord!
Great are you, Lord!

He Is Exalted

Words and Music by Twila Paris

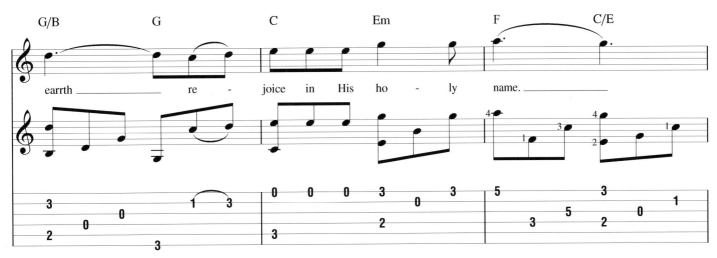

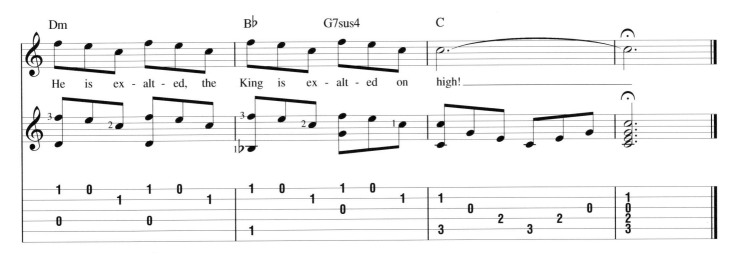

The Heart of Worship

Words and Music by Matt Redman

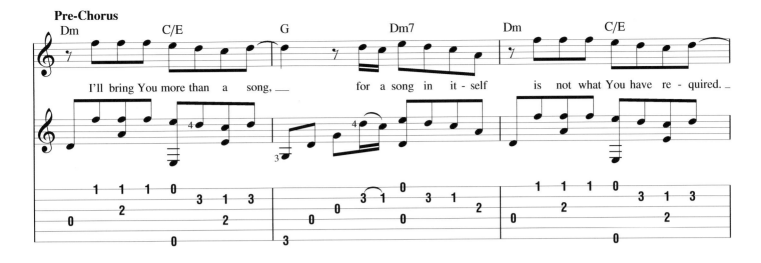

Pre-Chorus

I'll bring You more than a song, for a song in it - self is not what You have re - quired.

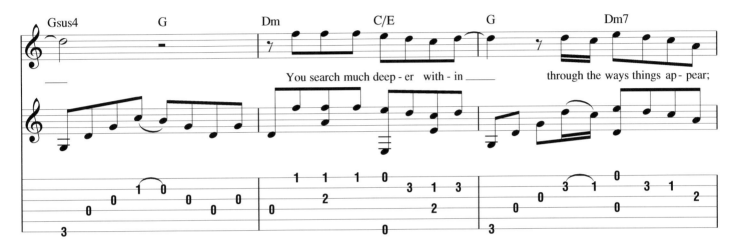

You search much deep - er with - in through the ways things ap - pear;

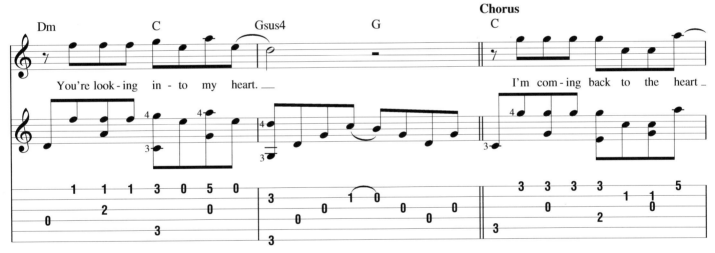

You're look - ing in - to my heart. I'm com - ing back to the heart

Chorus

of wor - ship, and it's all a - bout You, all a - bout You, Je - sus.

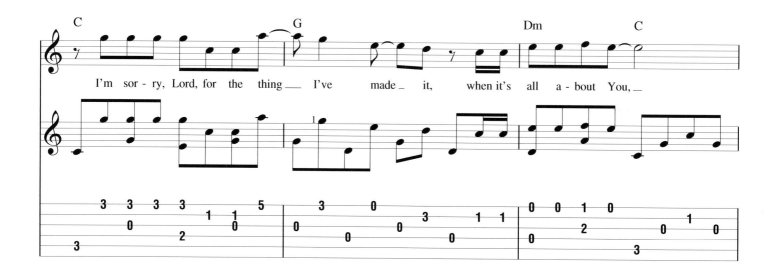

I'm sor - ry, Lord, for the thing ___ I've made ___ it, when it's all a - bout You, ___

all a - bout You, ___ Je - sus.

Additional Lyrics

2. King of endless worth, no one could express
   How much You deserve.
   Though I'm weak and poor, all I have is Yours,
   Ev'ry single breath.

Here I Am to Worship

Words and Music by Tim Hughes

Verse
Moderately

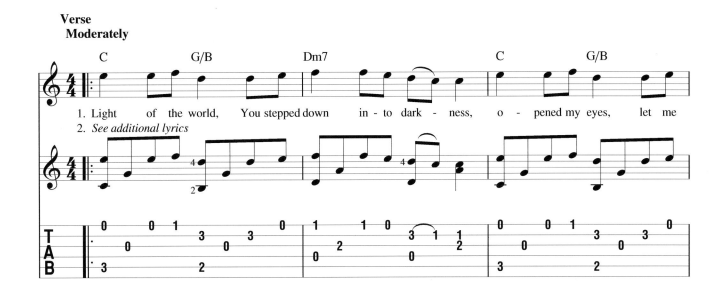

1. Light of the world, You stepped down in-to dark - ness, o - pened my eyes, let me
2. *See additional lyrics*

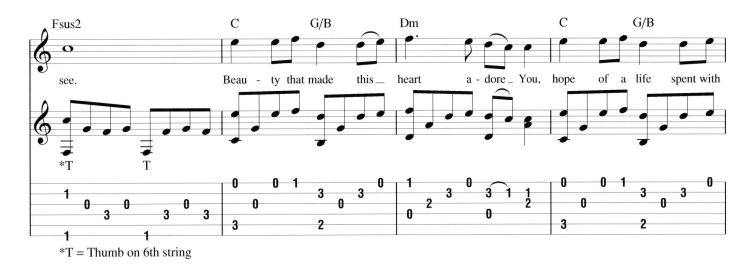

see. Beau - ty that made this heart a - dore You, hope of a life spent with

*T = Thumb on 6th string

Chorus

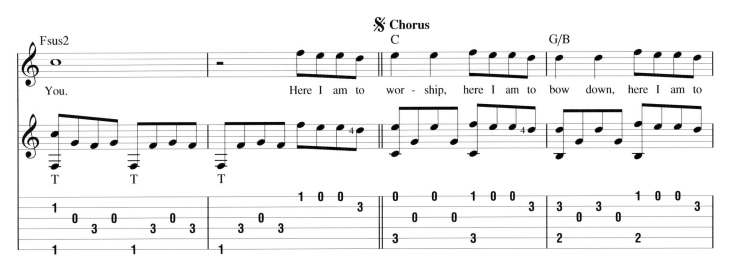

You. Here I am to wor - ship, here I am to bow down, here I am to

T   T   T

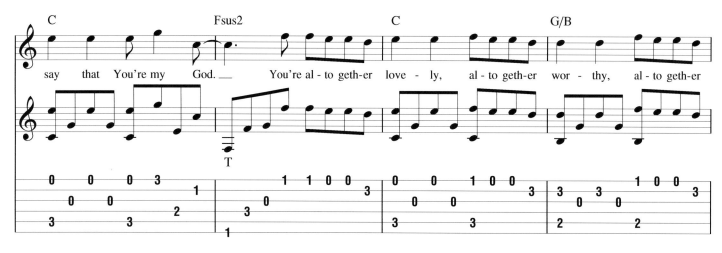

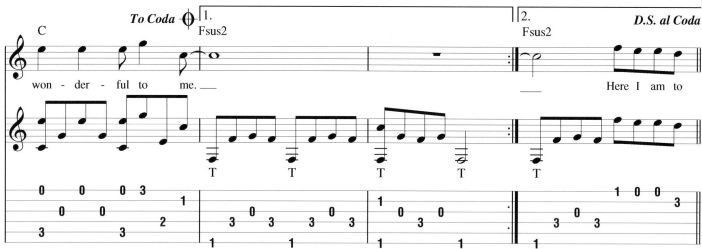

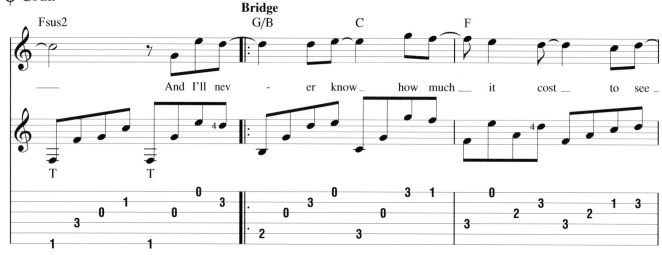

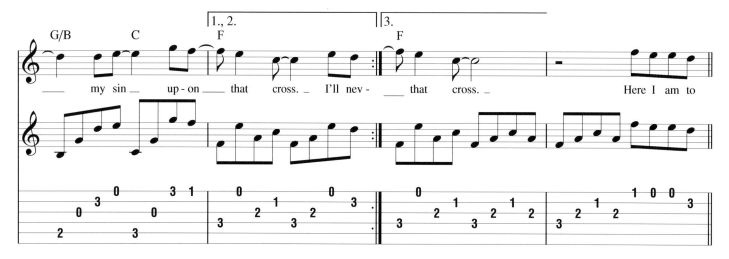

Outro-Chorus

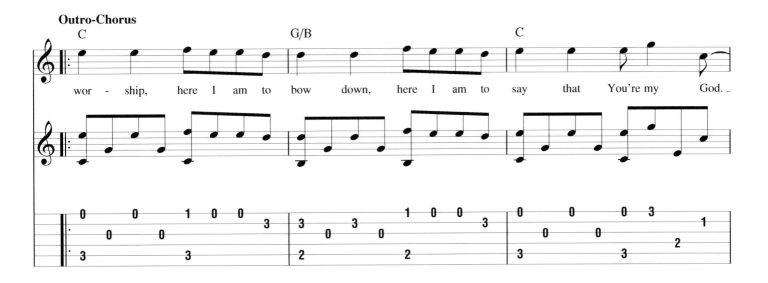

wor - ship, here I am to bow down, here I am to say that You're my God.

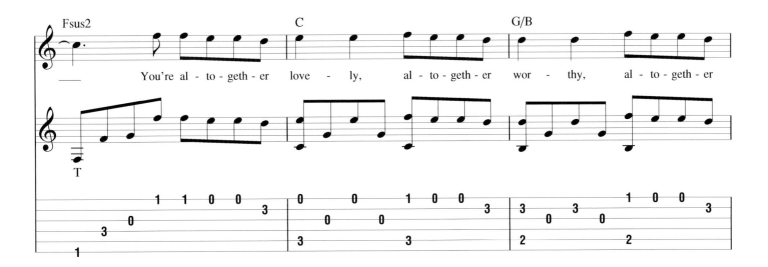

You're al - to - geth - er love - ly, al - to - geth - er wor - thy, al - to - geth - er

won - der - ful to me. Here I am to wor - ship.

Additional Lyrics

2. King of all days, oh, so highly exalted,
   Glorious in heaven above.
   Humbly You came to the earth You created,
   All for love's sake became poor.

Jesus, Name Above All Names

Words and Music by Naida Hearn

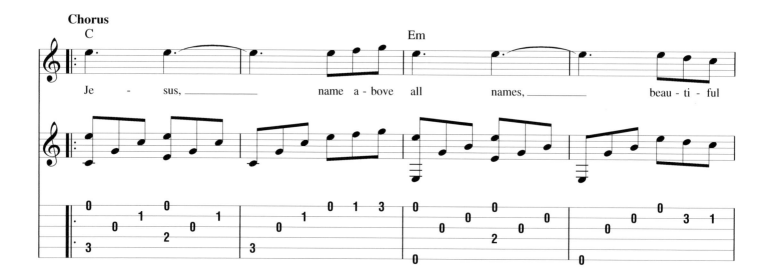

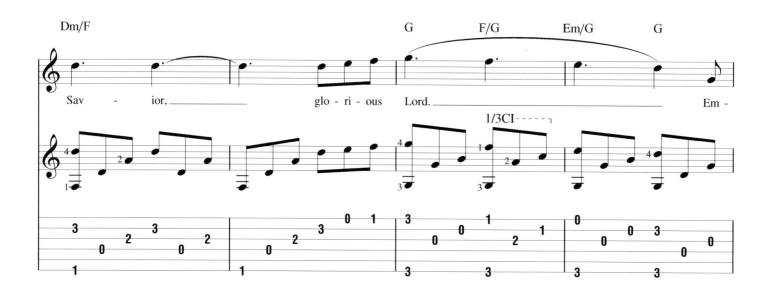

man - u - el, _____ God _ is with us, _____ bless - ed Re -

deem - er, _____ liv - ing Word. Word.

Je - sus, _____ name a - bove all names, _____

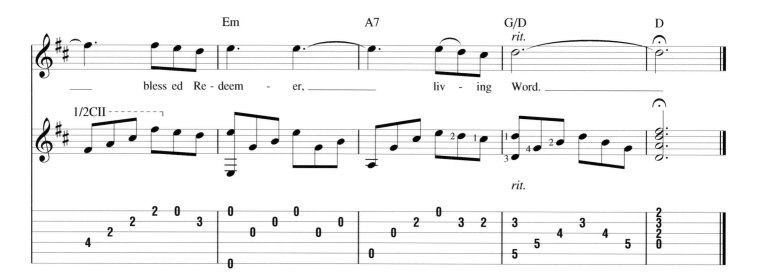

Shout to the Lord

Words and Music by Darlene Zschech

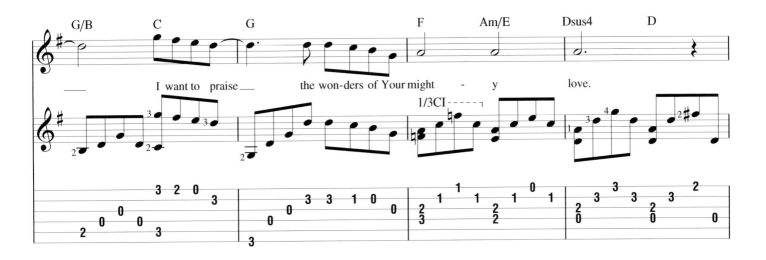

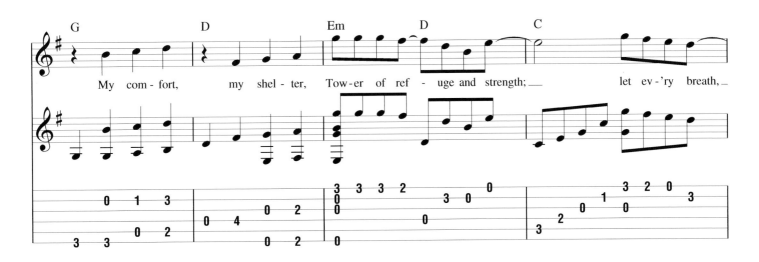

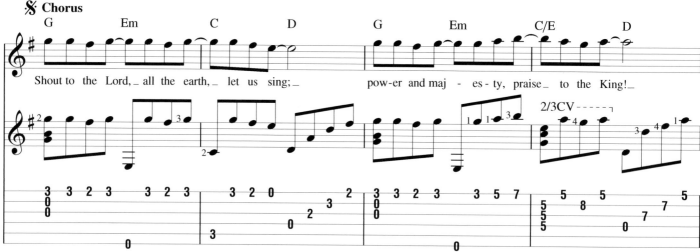

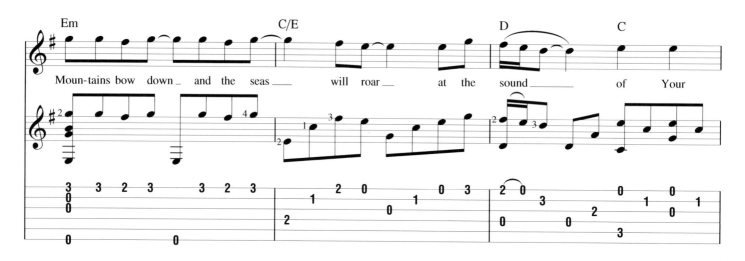

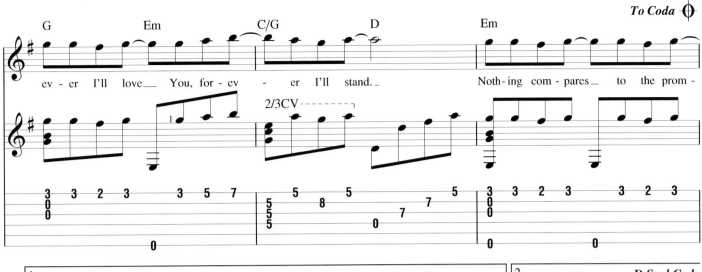
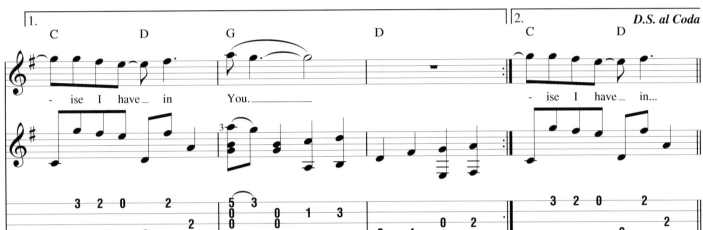
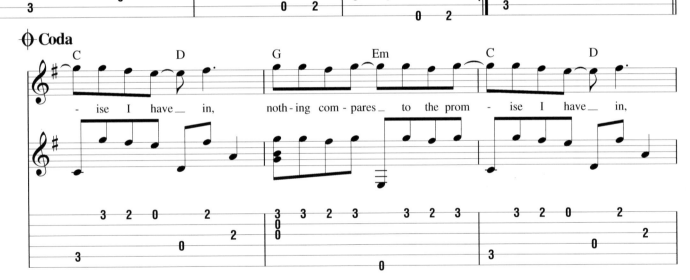
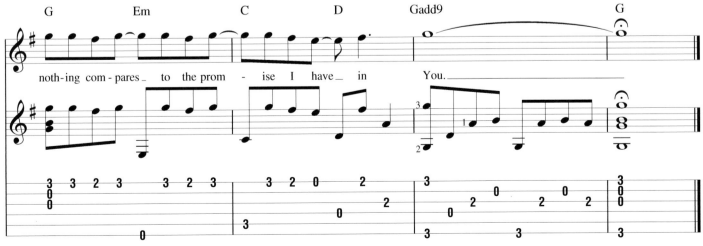

Oh Lord, You're Beautiful

Words and Music by Keith Green

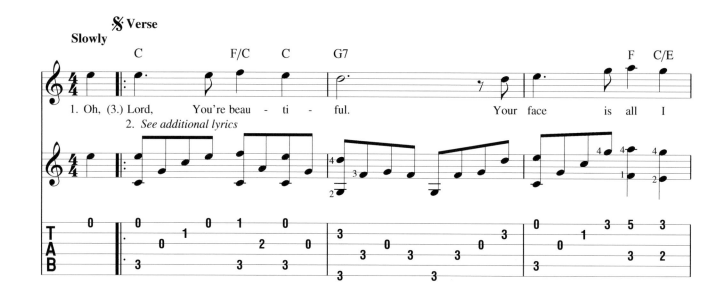

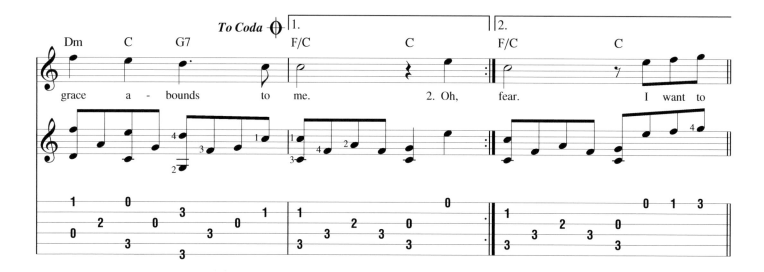

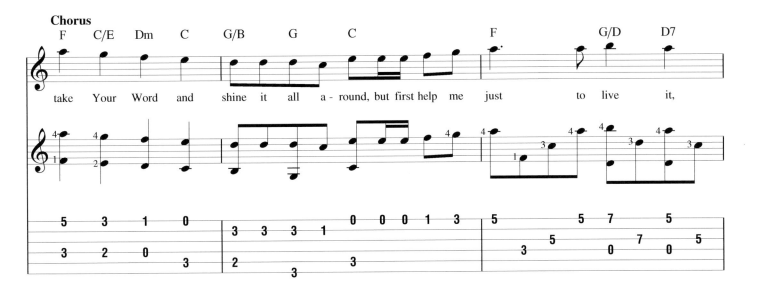

take Your Word and shine it all a - round, but first help me just to live it,

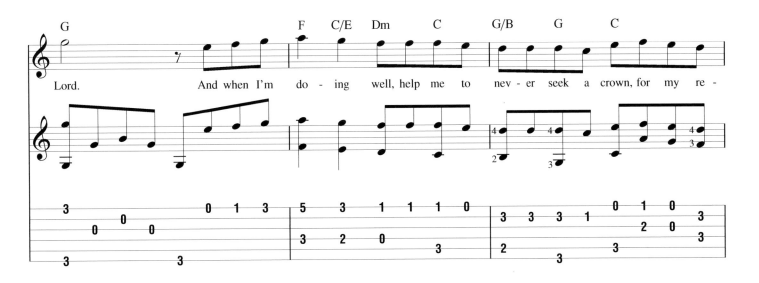

Lord. And when I'm do - ing well, help me to nev - er seek a crown, for my re -

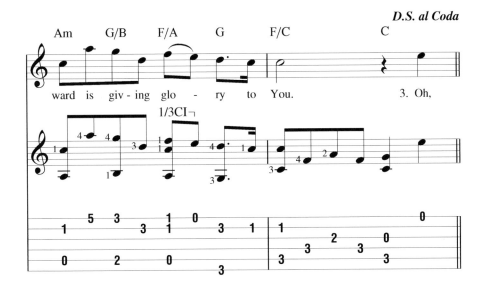

ward is giv - ing glo - ry to You. 3. Oh,

D.S. al Coda

ϕ **Coda**

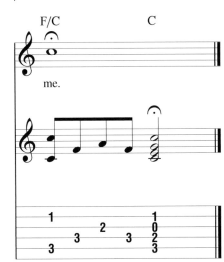

me.

Additional Lyrics

2. Oh, Lord, please light the fire
   That once burned bright and clear.
   Replace the lamp of my first love
   That burns with holy fear.

Open the Eyes of My Heart

Words and Music by Paul Baloche

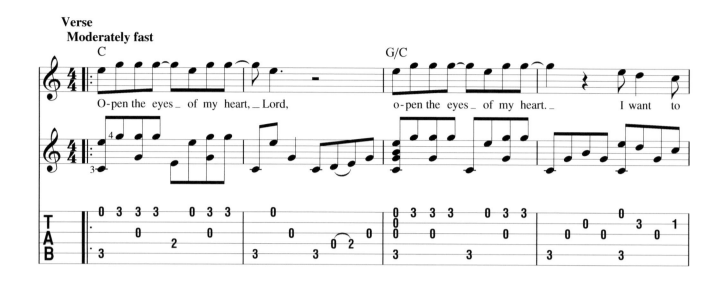

O-pen the eyes_ of my heart,_ Lord, o-pen the eyes_ of my heart._ I want to

see You,_ I want to see You._

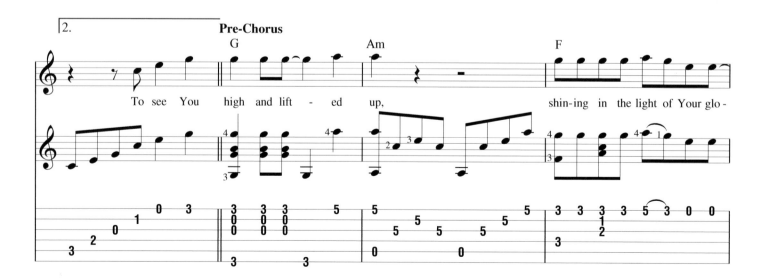

To see You high and lift - ed up, shin-ing in the light of Your glo-

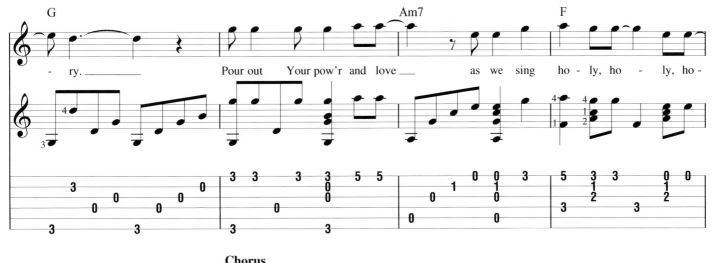

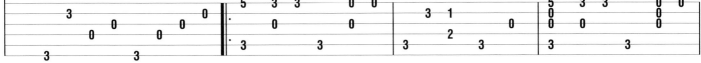

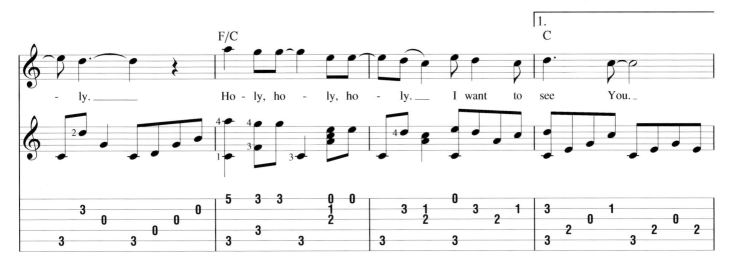

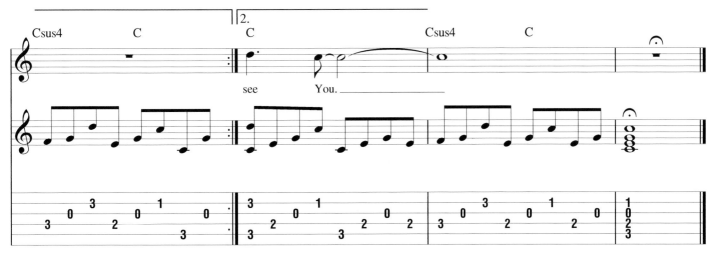

Shine, Jesus, Shine

Words and Music by Graham Kendrick

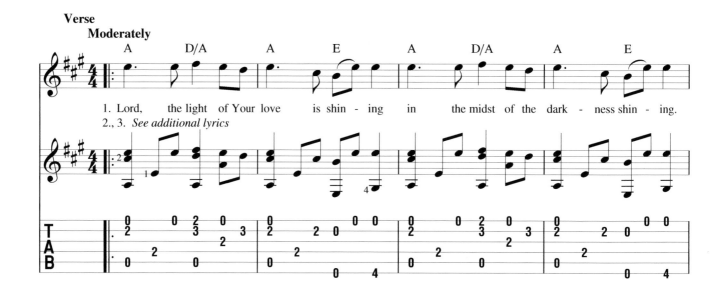

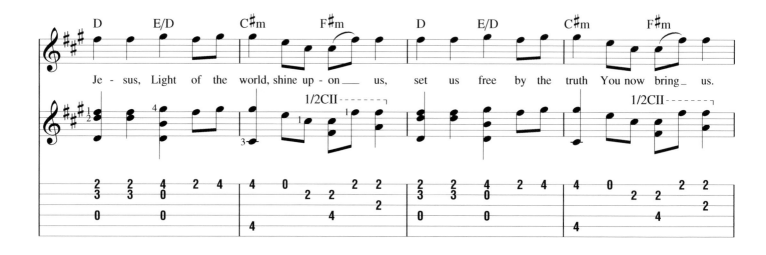

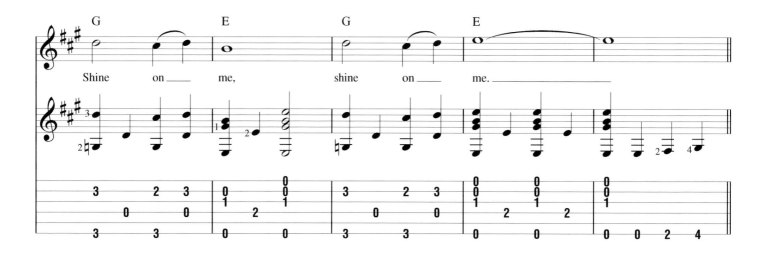

Chorus

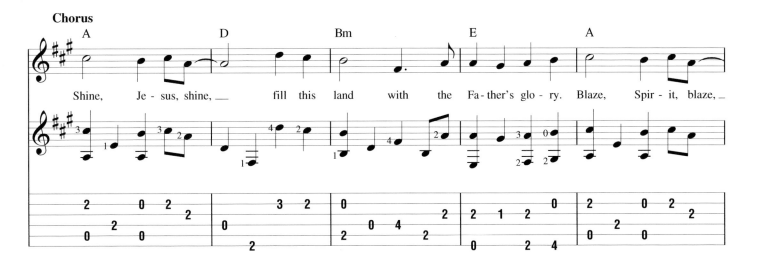

Shine, Je - sus, shine, ___ fill this land with the Fa - ther's glo - ry. Blaze, Spir - it, blaze, ___

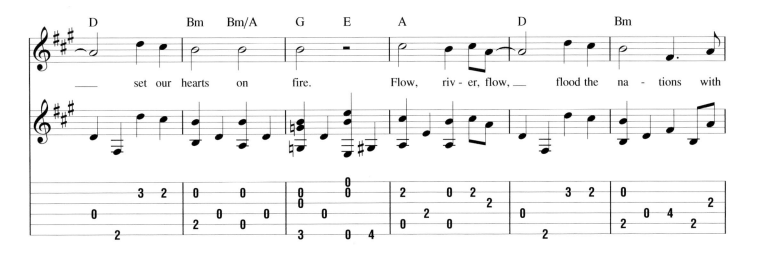

___ set our hearts on fire. Flow, riv - er, flow, ___ flood the na - tions with

grace and mer - cy. Send forth Your Word, ___ Lord, and let there be light. light.

Additional Lyrics

2. Lord, I come to Your awesome presence
   From the shadows in Your radiance;
   By the blood I may enter Your brightness,
   Search me, try me, consume all my darkness.
   Shine on me, shine on me.

3. As we gaze on Your kingly brightness,
   So our faces display Your likeness;
   Ever changing from glory to glory,
   Mirrored here may our lives tell Your story.
   Shine on me, shine on me.

Step by Step

Words and Music by David Strasser "Beaker"

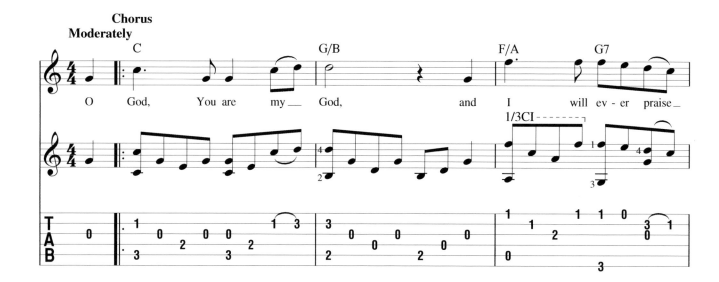

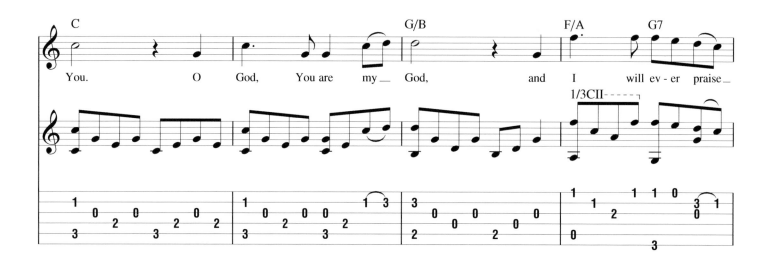

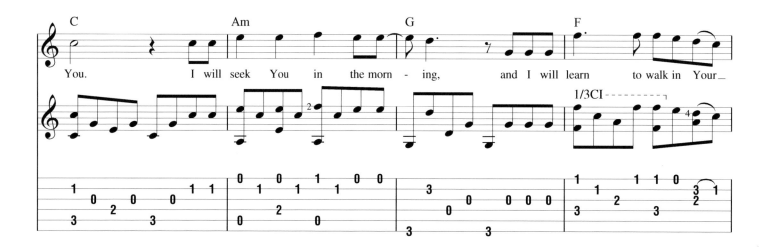

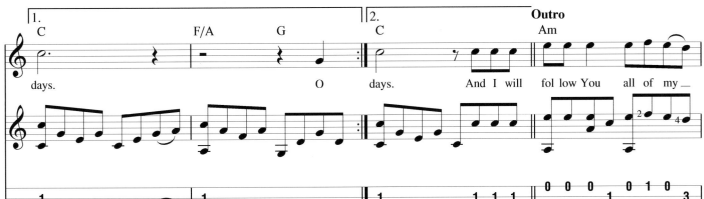

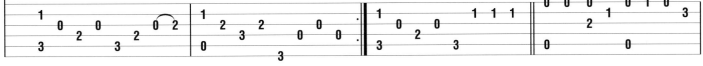

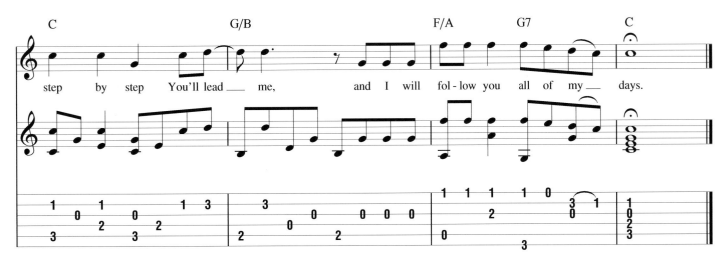

You Are My King
(Amazing Love)

Words and Music by Billy James Foote

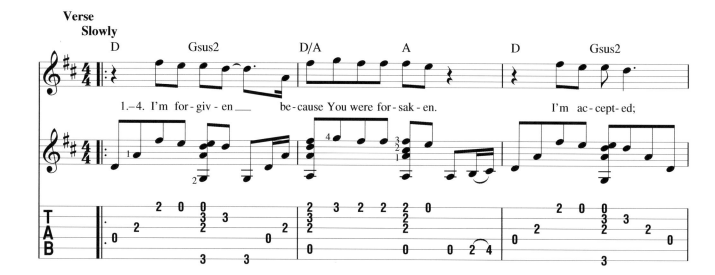

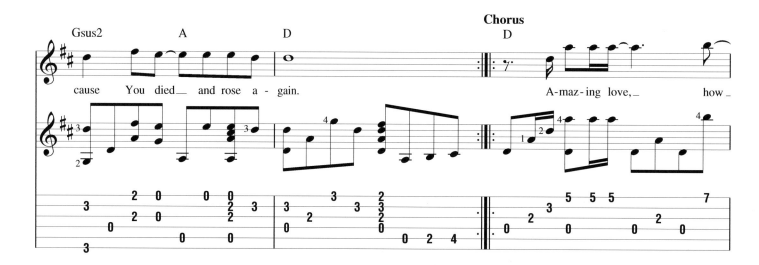

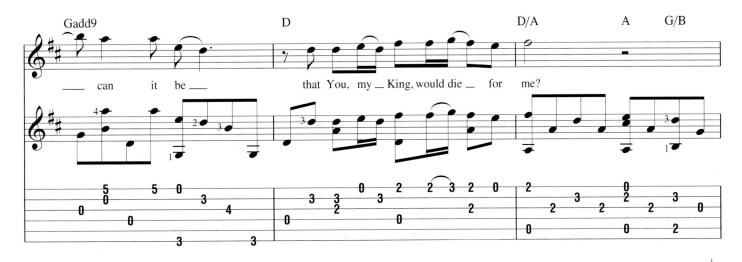

can it be ___ that You, my ___ King, would die ___ for me?

4th time, To Coda ⊕

A-maz-ing love, ___ I ___ know it's true; ___ it's my ___ joy to hon - or

1. You. You. In all ___ I ___ do, ___ I hon - or

Interlude

You. You are my King. ___

39

You ___ are my King. _ Je - sus, You ___ are my

D.C. al Coda
(take repeats)

King. _ ___ Je - sus, You ___ are my King. _

⊕ **Coda**

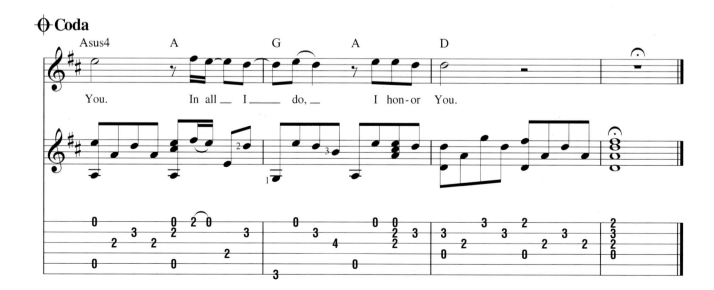

You. In all __ I ____ do, __ I hon - or You.